Participant's Guide

HALF

Changing Your Life Plan
from Success to Significance

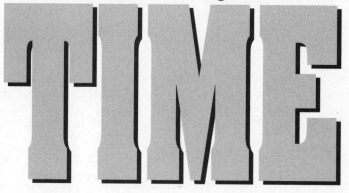

TIME

Participant's Guide

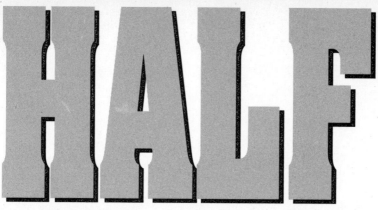

HALF

*Changing Your Life Plan
from Success to Significance*

TIME

Five Sessions Based on the Best-Selling Book by

BOB BUFORD

Participant's Guide written with Stephen and
Amanda Sorenson

ZondervanPublishingHouse
Grand Rapids, Michigan

Contents

Introduction

Something different begins to happen in our lives as we approach the special time that Bob Buford calls *halftime*. It's as if we've come to the end of a row and can't plow any further. It's time for something new. And it can be unsettling. That's why Buford's first book, *Halftime*, and his later book, *Game Plan*, have struck a chord with people from many walks of life and socioeconomic backgrounds who find themselves asking questions about the meaning and significance of their lives.

This study series is based on Buford's metaphor of a football game or any sport that divides its play into two halves. The playing field is the world in which we live. Halftime is the opportunity, after some of our life has passed, to evaluate what has taken place during the first half and to choose which new goals and dreams we may want to pursue during the second half of our lives.

The reality of the game of life, whether we like to admit it or not, is that the clock is running. What once looked like an eternity ahead of us is now within reach. Although we don't fear the end of the game, we do want to make sure that we finish well, that we leave something behind that no one can take away from us. This video and discussion series will help us discover significance and chart a course that will make the second half of our lives the best half.

1

Welcome to Halftime

The real test of a man [or woman] is not when he plays the role that he wants for himself, but when he plays the role destiny has for him.

Vaclav Havel

QUESTIONS TO THINK ABOUT

1. How would you define *success?*

2. How would you describe the relationship between success-fully earning a living and successfully using one's gifts, strengths, and abilities to create a significant life?

3. Which things do you consider to be truly significant—worth living or dying for?

VIDEO NOTES

Halftime: Is it time for something new?

Incidents that encourage reevaluation

Questions of significance

Sensing the start of a new season

The two final questions:

What did you do about Jesus?

What did you do with what Jesus gave you — your aptitudes, abilities, experiences, and resources?

VIDEO HIGHLIGHTS

1. Do you now have a better idea of what halftime is? Let's come up with a working definition.

2. Which of the people interviewed in the video segment described some of what you have felt or experienced? In what ways are they similar to or different from you?

3. Which thoughts and emotions surfaced as you watched this video segment? What surprised you or stood out above the rest? Be honest!

4. Do you believe that the second half of our lives should be the best half—that it can be, in fact, a personal renaissance? Why or why not?

HALFTIME CLIP

Halftime is the opportunity, after some of our life has passed, to evaluate what has taken place during the first half and to choose which new goals and dreams we may want to pursue during the second half of our lives.

—BOB BUFORD

LARGE GROUP EXPLORATION

Signals That Call for Our Attention

As we've seen, men and women who are in or are approaching halftime ask questions relating to their goals and life pursuits. They question perspectives and attitudes they have held for years. Previous goals and ways of doing things are no longer working as well as they used to. Let's explore some of the signals that indicate someone is in, or is approaching, halftime.

1. What external circumstances can arise that force us to reevaluate our priorities during midlife?

2. What symptoms of internal restlessness may prompt us to reevaluate our priorities?

3. How does the way we view our jobs today differ from the perspective of previous generations, particularly those of our grandparents or great-grandparents?

4. Describe, using your life or the life of someone you know, the visible signs that a person is not pleased with the way his or her life is going.

5. Sometimes, when people feel bored or ineffective and wonder if this is all there is, they ignore the inner voice that urges them to stop and explore their unfulfilled dreams and deepest hopes. Why do people ignore the halftime issues, and what happens when they do?

Pause for Personal Reflection

Now it's time to pause to think quietly about the signals of coming change in our lives that demand our attention.

What signals in my life may be indicating that I am in, or am approaching, halftime? How might my spouse, a family member, or a close friend answer this question?

What gives my life meaning?

Which of my dreams and hopes haven't been fulfilled yet?

What are the possible consequences if I were to reorder my life so that it would have greater significance?

HALFTIME CLIP

I knew **what** *I believed, but I didn't really know what I planned to* **do** *about what I believed. I was gripped with an unformed but very compelling idea that I should make my life truly productive, not merely profitable.*

—BOB BUFORD

SMALL GROUP EXPLORATION

What's Really Important?

Many years ago, the prophet Elijah powerfully brought God's judgment to bear on the false prophets of King Ahab of Israel. After God had demonstrated his power and the false prophets had been killed, King Ahab and his idolatrous wife, Jezebel, were angry. So Elijah fled for his life into the desert, where he evaluated his life and decided it was too tough to live. "I have had enough, Lord," he said. Then God spoke to him and asked him what he was doing in the desert. The prophet then spilled out his woes to God, and God responded.

1. Read 1 Kings 19:11–16 and answer the following questions.

    a. Often we pay attention to crises in our lives that force change, but we don't listen to the gentle whisper such as the one God provided Elijah. Why is it so hard for us to hear the whisper?

    b. If we took more time to listen to our gentle whispers—the thoughts, feelings, inner promptings, words of God—that seem to come during times of reflection and reevaluation, what might the consequences be?

2. How important is it for us to have an eternal perspective through which to view the goals and activities—and even the crises—of our lives?

3. What does it really mean to "have it all," to be "successful" in this life?

4. Why do we tend to put off thinking about whether the way we are living life right now is the best way for us to live?

5. In John 10:10, Jesus preached that he, the Good Shepherd, had come to earth so that his followers, the sheep, might "have life, and have it to the full."

    a. What do you think Jesus meant by having life "to the full"?

b. Does this verse indicate that Jesus planned to lead his people to restrictive, unrewarding places, or to places of significance? Why?

Pause for Personal Reflection

Now it's time to pause to evaluate what's really important in our lives.

What obstacles do I need to overcome in order to pay closer attention to my deepest longings? To the nudgings of God?

In light of my definition of success, am I truly successful? Am I living life to the full? Why or why not?

In what ways is my view of success changing? Is success as important to me as it once was?

Am I living a balanced life? Which priorities deserve more time?

HALFTIME CLIP

When it comes to having a better second half than the first, it doesn't matter whether you're a millionaire CEO, a high-paid lawyer, or a teacher. What's important is that you start by discovering the way God built you so you can use your uniquely developed talents for him. **—BOB BUFORD**

GROUP DISCUSSION

1. In what ways has what we have seen and discussed together today changed your definition of success?

2. The Scripture passage about Elijah that we read in our small groups shows that just when Elijah thought he was spent, used up, and ready for permanent retirement, God spoke to him in a whisper and gave him something important to do! What does this story say to you as you approach halftime?

3. So far, what are your thoughts about halftime? Are you encouraged? Apprehensive? Curious?

HALFTIME PERSPECTIVE

First-Half versus Halftime

The following chart, which is not pictured in the video, illustrates some of the differences that often exist between the first half of our lives and halftime.

Typical First-Half Pursuits and Challenges	Typical Halftime Questions and Issues
Obtaining an education.	What should I do with what I've learned? Have I done enough—in my family, my community, my church?
Getting married or building relationships with friends.	Am I able to devote time to the people who are most important to me? To help them become all they can be? To reach out to others?
Building a career and striving to move upward, trying to provide for the family. Having good intentions.	Are these long hours really worth the price? And now that I'm here, is this where I want to be? I want more than success; I want significance. I'm successful, fortunate, and yet frustratingly unfulfilled.
Acquiring material things to help make life's journey more comfortable.	May have lived more than half my life. What am I going to leave behind of lasting value? Do I really need more stuff?
Juggling many priorities—how to be with friends and family yet expend oneself in the adventure of developing a career.	What's *really* important? Maybe it's time to take a breather and reevaluate things. How would I like my life to be different—if I'm really honest?

Experiencing pain: divorce, addiction, guilt, loneliness, wayward children, job loss, cancer, etc.	How can I use the great learning experiences I've had and wisdom I've gained to make a difference in this world—to draw me closer to people and to God?
Determining what I have to work with—my gifts, abilities, knowledge, experiences.	I know quite a bit about what I have to work with; now it's time to choose strategically how to use what I have.
Choosing challenges and new horizons that fit the game plan.	Now I can build on the past to create new challenges, new horizons that reflect my new goals and to discover what it means to be open to what God wants me to do.
Marching ahead, pursuing the goals, playing hard.	I just can't keep playing the game the way I've been playing. But I want the second half of my life to be even better than the first.
Trying to figure out what to believe spiritually. If this leads to becoming a Christian, then developing a belief system.	I want to figure out what to *do* with what I believe. I want my faith to be lived out through action that is built on my faith and beliefs.
Getting involved in activities and figuring out how life works.	I dare to believe that what I ultimately leave behind will be more important than anything I could have achieved during the first half of my life.

ACTION POINTS

What will you commit to do as a result of what you have discovered during this session?

1. Today a growing number of men and women in midlife are asking themselves, "What do I want to do now that I've grown up? Is this all there is?" Bob Buford identifies this stage of life as *halftime.* It is the opportunity, after some of our life has passed, to evaluate what has taken place during the first half and to choose which goals and dreams we may want to pursue during the second half of our lives. Halftime is the start of an exciting journey that can take us past success and lead us toward significance.

    Most of us want not merely to be remembered but to be remembered for something significant. Here's one way to discover what is truly significant to you:

    Using just one phrase or sentence, write out what you would like written on your gravestone.

    Allow what you write to express the goals to which you will be committed until you rest beneath that gravestone, the purpose and passion that will characterize you from this day forward. (If you are not yet sure what to write, leave this question unanswered and come back to it later.)

2. Bob Buford believes that God has prepared each of us "to do a good work" and that when we reach the midpoint of life many of us can choose how we will spend the second part of our lives. Will we keep doing the same things in the same ways? Will we continue to pursue success and strive for more material possessions? Or will we courageously step out of the comfort zone and discover our God-given calling? Will we allow God to guide us toward something more? Will we use halftime to consciously evaluate where we have been and perhaps set our course in a new direction?

    Set aside at least one hour this week during which, away from most or all distractions, you can begin thinking about the following:

    1. **Take an inventory of your unique gifts, resources, abilities, and experiences. (Examples might include the opportunity to influence people, time to pray, a strong character developed through suffering, a love for children, material resources, a level of expertise in a unique skill.)**

2. Now write down ways in which you might be able to use the above inventory during the second half of your life. Remember, no matter where you live, who you know, what you do, or how much money you make, God has a special calling for you to fulfill right where you are.

HALFTIME CLIP

I knew I was successful in my early thirties, and I was very troubled by it, of all things. I describe it in Halftime *as "success panic," where you actually get where you want to go!* It's like a dog chasing a car and catching up with it and getting a bite of the tire—it's frightening in some ways. It caused me to sit down under a tree with my Daytimer and say, "What's really important? Is this it?"   —BOB BUFORD

HALFTIME DRILL

Take Stock of Your First Half

The following questions may help you take stock of your first half as you prepare for a better second half.

1. For what do you want to be remembered? Describe how your life would look if it turned out just the way you wished.

2. How much money is enough? If you have more than enough, what purpose does the excess serve? If you have less than enough, what are you willing to do to correct that?

3. How do you feel about your career? Is this what you want to be doing with your life ten years from now?

4. Are you living a balanced life? Which important elements of your life deserve more time? Which elements would you like to eliminate?

5. Are you becoming the person you really want to be? If not, what are you willing to do about it?

6. What is the primary loyalty in your life?

7. Where do you seek inspiration and mentors for your life?

8. What kinds of relationships do you want with your family and friends?

9. What pursuits have dominated your life thus far? In what ways have you benefited from them? What have been the drawbacks?

10. If your life story to date indicates what lies ahead for you, what do you think your future holds?

HALFTIME PERSPECTIVE

A Model for Our Spiritual Journey

In his first book, *Halftime*, Bob Buford uses the following baseball diagram to illustrate a person's spiritual journey. Perhaps it may help you clarify where you are—which base you are on or headed toward.

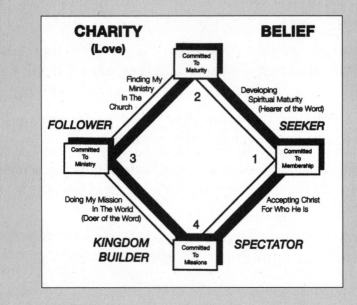

The First Half: Developing Faith and Belief

1. Getting to first base. Here, a spectator who has been on the sidelines accepts Jesus Christ for who he is through a simple act of faith. This act of faith changes the person from being a spectator to engaging his or her rational and emotional senses on the journey toward personal spiritual growth.

2. Moving to second base. The new Christian makes a commitment to developing spiritual maturity. This includes gaining an understanding of what faith in God really means. For many people, including Bob Buford, this part of the journey focuses on belief—the internally held belief system that grows the more they study the Bible and its unique truths concerning life and God.

Bob Buford, in *Halftime*, reported that George Gallup Jr. says 84 percent of Americans declare themselves to be Christians. Yet there doesn't seem to be corresponding evidence of Christlikeness in our society. Bob believes this is because many Christians are "stuck somewhere between first and second base."

The Second Half: Doing Good Works That Come from Faith and Belief

3. Reaching third base. Here, the person:

- Moves from spiritual maturity and developing a personal belief system to releasing seeds of creativity and energy that God has implanted in him or her.
- Waters and cultivates these seeds so they will become fruitful.
- Starts being committed to expressing love, to investing his or her gifts in service to other people. The resulting good works are an extension of the person's beliefs and give these beliefs integrity.
- Expresses his or her faith in Jesus by reaching out to other people, in the power of God, through a church or parachurch organization.
- Assumes individual responsibility, taking steps to be involved in people's lives.

4. Heading toward home plate. This person:

- Is discovering God's specific mission for him or her—what the Greeks called destiny.
- Is actively living out his or her faith in the everyday world.
- Is sharing the love and good news of Jesus with other people.
- Is committed to making a difference in the world through God's power.

2

Exploring Possibilities

Beware the urge to get away from it all. That is not what the second half is all about. I know people who are well into their second halves who are still working at the same job they started with and who will be there to get the gold watch. The key to a successful second half is not a change of jobs; it is a change of heart— a change in the way you view the world and order your life.

Bob Buford

QUESTIONS TO THINK ABOUT

1. Sometimes what we say we believe appears to be quite different from the way we actually live and the choices we make. In what ways have you found this to be true in your life and the lives of other people?

2. How important is it to become personally involved in causes we really believe in? Why?

3. What do you think a person needs to do to start thinking beyond what is and begin dreaming about what could be? What enables a person to explore the possibilities and view life as an epic—a grand, ambitious journey that leads toward significance?

VIDEO NOTES, PART 1

Being a hero

Bob and Tina Muzikowski—choosing significance

Personal involvement

Personal sacrifice

Halftime—a change of heart

VIDEO HIGHLIGHTS

1. What do you think of the life Bob and Tina have chosen to pursue?

2. Do you long to experience the passion and purpose in life that Bob and Tina seem to have? Describe what that passion and purpose might look like in your life.

3. In what ways does Bob and Tina's response to the halftime process challenge you to evaluate your life and potential journey toward significance?

4. As you watched this video segment, what ideas came to mind regarding what you could do during your second half?

LARGE GROUP EXPLORATION

Pursuing Something Larger Than Our Personal Concerns

A hero is someone who gives himself or herself over to something larger than his or her personal concerns. In the Bible we find many stories of heroes—men and women who accepted the calling, the destiny, that God had for them. These men and women made the personal sacrifices necessary to pursue their unique calling, even when it led into previously uncharted territory. Let's read about a few of these heroes of the Bible and see what we learn about how they each recognized their calling and responded to it.

1. Abram (whose name was later changed to Abraham)—Genesis 12:1–5.

2. Moses—Exodus 3:1–4, 7–12; 4:20 (If time permits, see 3:13–4:19 also.)

3. Mordecai's adopted daughter, Esther, the Jewish woman who became the wife of King Xerxes of Persia—Esther 2:17–20; 3:8–11; 4:1, 5–16

4. Paul—Acts 9:1–6, 10–22

5. Daniel—Daniel 6:6–27

Pause for Personal Reflection

Now it's time to pause to consider God's calling for each of us and the ways in which he might be revealing it.

Do I believe that God has a calling—a specific purpose—for everyone? If so, how important is it for me to discover and pursue my calling?

Have I taken God's calling for my life into account when I have made significant plans in the past? Why or why not?

In what ways might God be revealing his calling for me? What do I think that calling might be?

HALFTIME DRILL

Leading Questions for Exploring Your Calling

In his book *Halftime,* Bob Buford reminds us that "halftime is more than putting your feet up and meditating. It's more than time away to think, pray, and play. A successful halftime needs some structure. Set an agenda that will help you 'walk' through the important issues. Such an agenda will indeed include time to pray and listen, to read the Scriptures, and to think, but it should also include some deliberate questions."

The following questions may guide you as you begin to explore what your God-given calling may be.

1. What is my passion?

2. Where do I belong?

3. What do I believe? And what will I do about what I believe?

4. How am I wired?

Continued on next page...

5. What are my core values? And to what degree should I make key decisions based on these values?

6. What are my aspirations?

7. What do I have to do, learn, and/or change to become capable of living up to the demands I place on myself and to fulfill my expectations of life?

8. For what regrets or mistakes do I need to forgive myself — and view as markers from which I can learn valuable lessons?

9. What do I want to be doing in ten years? In twenty years?

10. What gifts has God given me that have been perfected over time? What gifts has God given me that I'm unable to use?

11. What changes might I need to make in order to better align my job and career with my true self?

12. If I remain on the same track, pursuing the same types of things I am pursuing today, where will I end up?

SMALL GROUP EXPLORATION

Needed: A Change of Heart

In the video segment, Bob Buford said, "The key to a successful second half is not a change of jobs. It's a change of heart." Let's take a few minutes to consider what kind of change of heart leads to a significant second half.

1. The changes Bob and Tina Muzikowski made in their lives sprang out of a change of heart. Bob cut back on his hours as a benefits planner and agent for Northwestern Mutual and earns less than he used to. To be a part of the community they felt led to serve, they moved from the suburbs and into the city. In light of these changes and the challenges they have encountered, why was the change of heart he and Tina experienced so important?

2. In the Bible, the word *heart* is used to describe the deepest part of a person—the core of his or her being. Read each of the following verses and note what they teach us about the human heart and what brings about a change of heart.

Scripture	The Truth About the Human Heart
Matthew 6:19–21	
Matthew 22:37–40 (also Deut. 6:5–6)	

Continued on next page...

Scripture	The Truth About the Human Heart
Hebrews 4:12	
Hebrews 4:13	
Jeremiah 17:10	
Proverbs 21:2	

Pause for Personal Reflection

Now it's time to pause to consider where our hearts are focused.

As I read the verses describing the human heart, what did I discover about my heart?

What is the true focus of my heart?

Which aspects of my life—my thoughts, my words, my actions—fall into place according to that focus?

VIDEO NOTES, PART 2

Lillian Barger—exploring a parallel career

Bill Simon—in training to do God's will

Margaret Dye—listening for God's purpose

VIDEO HIGHLIGHTS

1. In what ways did you identify with Lillian, Bill, and Margaret as they talked about their halftime explorations and discoveries? What impact did their experiences have on you?

2. Rena Pederson observed that the halftime process is often different for women than it is for men. In what ways might halftime be different? In what ways might it be similar?

HALFTIME CLIP

Some people make the mistake of using halftime to fantasize, wistfully projecting various images of themselves into unrealistic situations that will never happen. But getting ready for a better second half is not daydreaming. You need to honestly face the tough, nitty-gritty questions about finances, other family members, and long-range goals. And when you do ask the hard questions, don't fudge on the answers. To make the second half better than the first, you need to discover the real you. **—BOB BUFORD**

PERSONAL EXPLORATION

Barriers That Hold Us Back

Regardless of where we live, how much money we make, what talents we have, and even the mistakes we have made, we can give ourselves permission to be open to new possibilities that lead toward significance. Yet many of us find it difficult to actually live as if new possibilities are available to us. We may have lots to say when we're asked what we're missing in our lives, what we value, or what we might like to be doing in five to ten years, but we fail to set aside the time and energy to reflect on these possibilities and pursue them.

1. Consider the following common attitudes and beliefs that can negatively impact our ability to dream about new opportunities and pursue a significant second half. Check off the barriers that are most challenging to you and note the impact they have had on your life.

    ❑ I am overly influenced by other people's (or society's) expectations of who I should be. As a result, I _____

    _____.

    ❑ Financial concerns are very important to me. I have too little money (or too much money to put at risk) to cut back on my schedule and pursue some dream that I hope will lead to significance. As a result, I _____

    _____.

❑ I like knowing what's ahead, so I stay on the present course. I don't like the uncertainty and fear that come when I start thinking about different opportunities for the future. It's too confusing. As a result, I _____

_____.

❑ I have so much to do today that I can't take time out to think about future possibilities. Thinking about the future doesn't accomplish anything for me today. As a result, I

_____

_____.

❑ I've been successful, but I've failed God and hurt other people in the process. I'm not so sure I deserve a better second half. As a result, I _____.

_____

❑ God might have something for me to do, but I can't see my gifts, talents, knowledge, experiences, or training leading to anything big, exciting, or significant. As a result, I

_____

_____.

❑ When I no longer have what it takes to stay on top of my game, I'll be miserable. Life will be downhill from that point on. As a result, I _____

_____.

❑ I'd like to do something significant, but not if I'm going to lose any of the power and prestige I enjoy today. As a result, I _____

_____.

❑ I'd like to do something significant, and I have several areas of interest, but there's nothing compelling that I feel led to pursue. As a result, I _____

_____.

2. Write down any additional barriers that are keeping you from exploring the opportunity to discover a significant second half.

3. For each barrier you checked, write down specific actions you could take to begin facing and overcoming that barrier.

4. What will be the consequences if you do not deal with these barriers soon?

HALFTIME CLIP

For me, the transition into the after- noon of life was a time for reorder- ing my time and my treasure, for reconfiguring my values and my vision of what life could be. It repre- sented more than a renewal; it was a new begin- ning. It was more than a reality check; it was a fresh and leisurely look into the holiest chamber of my own heart, affording me, at last, an opportu- nity to respond to my soul's deepest longings.
—BOB BUFORD

HALFTIME PERSPECTIVE

A Hope for the Future

The halftime process is certainly challenging and at times even frightening. Yet when we seek to know God and to follow his leading in life, we can explore the possibilities and approach the uncertainties of halftime with hope and confidence because God promises to be with us. Notice the following promises and take heart as you explore new possibilities for the second half of your life!

God's Promises	Scripture
God is with us always, offering guidance and counsel as he leads us to our ultimate destination.	Psalm 73:23–24
God is attentive to the prayers of righteous people who believe in him.	1 Peter 3:12
We don't need to chase after the necessities of life. God, who believes each of us is valuable, will care for and meet the needs of those who seek his kingdom and his righteousness above all else.	Matthew 6:25–26; 31–33
We can hold on to our hope with confidence because God will remain faithful to his promises no matter what.	Hebrews 10:23
God has plans for his people—plans for their benefit that give them a hope and a future.	Jeremiah 29:11
God has created his people to do good works that he prepares in advance for them to do.	Ephesians 2:10
God is our refuge and strength, always available to help us.	Psalm 46:1

GROUP DISCUSSION

1. Now that you've seen some people who are discovering their callings and committing themselves to doing something significant during the second half of life, something that wells up from deep within themselves, what do you find yourself thinking about or feeling? Do you feel sad about what you haven't done? Have you been inspired to start thinking in new directions? To do something?

2. What did you discover about the process of making significant changes in life as you listened to the experiences of people you saw in the video segment?

3. Let's review some of the reasons why people who are in or are approaching halftime should evaluate the possibilities that can lead to a significant second half.

4. What are the differences in attitude, lifestyle, and future benefits between simply doing something you enjoy and giving yourself over to something larger than your personal concerns?

5. In light of what we've learned during this session, why is it important to take time to listen to God and be open to the implications of what he reveals as we explore our dreams and desires during the halftime process?

HALFTIME TIP

Which transition options below best fit your temperament and gifts?

- Keep doing what you are doing, but change the environment.
- Change what you are doing, but stay in the same environment.
- Turn an avocation into a career.
- Double-track (or even triple-track) in parallel careers (not hobbies).
- Keep doing what you are doing, even past retirement age.

ACTION POINTS

What will you commit to do as a result of what you have discovered during this session?

1. Halftime gives people in midlife the opportunity to explore possibilities, to realize that they can give themselves permission to dream about making changes, to look for ways in which they can discover and live out their calling based on who God created them to be.

    What steps are you willing to take to begin discovering the calling God has for your life? These steps may be as varied as "talking to my spouse about certain possibilities," "taking a class on _____," "taking a weekend away from everything just to think and dream," "volunteering at _____ for _____," or "reading that book I've always wanted to read."

    Write down these steps!

2. Halftime is a time to slow down, listen to God, and be open to the implications of what he reveals. Often, to listen to God, people need to take time out from the hustle and bustle of daily existence and find that place where the quiet voice of God is most audible.

What changes will you make in your routine that will give you more time to slow down and listen to God—and to your own dreams and desires for the future?

What is the best way for you to structure that time with God?

If nothing else, set aside at least one hour this week during which, away from most or all distractions, you can begin thinking about your halftime possibilities and listening for God's leading.

3. Halftime isn't about getting away from it all. It's about a change of heart that urges people to move beyond their personal concerns and to ask the challenging questions that will lead them on a journey toward significance. It's a time to dedicate themselves to something much bigger than themselves so they can fulfill God's special calling for their lives.

   How important is it to you to become involved in a cause much larger than your personal concerns? How would its importance change if you believed God was guiding you in that direction?

On what is your heart focused right now? Do you need to ask God to change your heart and reveal the larger cause to which he may be calling you?

To the best of your ability at this point, describe the larger cause that might play a role in a significant second half for you.

HALFTIME CLIP

Don't expect to solve all your first-half issues and plan for the second half in a few hours. For most people, halftime takes several months, even years. But it will never happen if we don't give it the time it deserves.

—BOB BUFORD

HALFTIME PERSPECTIVE

Guidelines for a Successful Halftime

Many times, a good second half depends on what is done during halftime. The following concepts helped Bob Buford prepare to launch into the second half of his life.

1. Make peace with your first-half issues. This doesn't mean that you are proud of all you've done or that you would change nothing in your life if you could. Any honest look back will recall several things you wish you had done differently. The key is to keep these things in perspective and to accept them as an inevitable part of growth.

2. Take time for the things that are really important. This requires a certain amount of discipline and time management, and there will be the tendency to view this as yet another appointment on your already overscheduled date book. But you can take the time. Konosuke Matsushita, chairman of the huge and highly successful Japanese electronics company bearing his last name, follows the practice, not uncommon in Asia, of retreating to his garden from time to time to live a contemplative and reflective life. And when he walks into a room, the awe is palpable. Without saying a word, he bespeaks a powerful centeredness and elegant reserve.

3. Be deliberate. Halftime is more than putting your feet up and meditating. It's more than time away to think, pray, and play. A successful halftime needs structure. Set an agenda that will help you walk through the important issues.

4. Share the journey. Bob Buford cannot imagine making his transition from the first half to the second without being accompanied on the journey by his wife. She asked questions, made suggestions, kept him honest. If your marriage is truly a partnership, it would be wrong to impose a whole new lifestyle on your spouse without his or her input. If you are not married, seek out an accountability partner who will listen, encourage, and help keep you on track.

Continued on next page...

5. Be honest. Getting ready for a better second half is not daydreaming. You need to honestly face the tough, nitty-gritty questions about finances, other family members, and long-range goals. When you ask the hard questions, don't fudge on the answers. Your second half will focus on your true self, so be honest enough to discover it.

6. Be patient. It took you the better part of two decades or longer to reach this point. You can't undo everything overnight. You will still have to go to work tomorrow. Bills will arrive in the mail. Clients will expect to have their calls returned. And a clear picture of what you should do with the second half of your life may not emerge anytime soon.

7. Have faith. For Christians, halftime is basically a time to answer the question, "What will I do about what I believe?" Begin to answer that by putting your faith to work, by trusting God to guide you. Listen to his voice through Scripture and the thoughts he brings to mind as you talk with him.

3

What's in the Box?

The thing is to understand myself, to see what God really wishes me to do ... to find the idea for which I can live and die.

Søren Kierkegaard

QUESTIONS TO THINK ABOUT

1. During our previous session, we talked about exploring possibilities that could lead to a significant second half. What are your feelings as you consider what would make your life significant?

2. As we consider the possibilities for a successful second half, why might it be important for each of us to narrow our focus and identify the one thing—the core value or belief, the primary loyalty, the overriding desire—that will provide purpose, direction, and motivation for the second half of our lives?

3. What are some of the things that motivate people, consciously or unconsciously, to pursue specific directions?

4. To what extent do our deepest spiritual values influence our motivation?

HALFTIME CLIP

When we look back on the twentieth century, the thing that is going to have the greatest impact is not going to be technology, as we now assume. Rather, it will be the fact that we have an infinite array of options.

—PETER DRUCKER

VIDEO NOTES

"What's in the box?"

Karol's discovery

Jim's discovery

Crises that lead us to ask the question, "What's in the box?"

VIDEO HIGHLIGHTS

1. Why is it important to discover the one thing in your box?

2. Karol Emmerich spoke of having inklings of profound boredom even though she lived a very successful and exciting life. In what ways have you experienced such inklings? What are your clues that life as you live it now isn't enough to satisfy you?

3. Jim Thweatt gets excited about helping kids who are headed for failure to stay in school, learn, and prosper. When he talks about these kids, it's easy to see where his treasure is. It is easy to see what is in his box. Why is what's in his box an important idea for Jim?

4. Like Tim Sambrano and Rogers Kirven, most of us think we will be satisfied and happy once we have successfully achieved our dreams. Yet they discovered the dark side of half-time—the frustration and uncertainty of living without direction, of living a life that lacks significance. What are the implications of their discovery for your life?

HALFTIME CLIP

Significance begins by stopping wherever you are in the journey to see what's in the box, and then reordering your life around its contents. **—BOB BUFORD**

LARGE GROUP EXPLORATION

Discovering What's in Our Box

We've seen a glimpse of how important it is for each of us to choose the one thing in our box—the one thing that will provide motivation and purpose for the second half of our lives. Some people choose family, money, or career. Bob Buford chose Jesus Christ. Regardless of what is, or has been, in our box, let's talk about the process of discovering what we really want to put into our box.

Perhaps we have made that choice already. Perhaps we have allowed other people or circumstances to make that choice for us. But it's never too late for each of us to evaluate what's in our box and see if what has been the one thing should stay there or be replaced.

1. What are some of the common beliefs and core values around which people build their lives?

2. Let's say person A decides that the one thing in his or her box is money—achieving financial freedom by a specific age. Person B, on the other hand, has put making a difference in the lives of disadvantaged young people in the box. Although individual situations obviously vary, let's consider some of the ways in which person A and person B might make different decisions in the following areas.

Decision Area	Person A: Financial Freedom	Person B: Helping Young People
Family Life Involvement		
Dedication to Career		
Use of Personal Time		
Use of Financial Resources		
Use of Talents		

3. What are some of the obstacles that may make it difficult for a person to put that one thing of his or her choosing into the box?

4. Do you think everyone who seriously evaluates what's in his or her box must also address such spiritual questions as, "Where is God in my life?" "What is God doing, and what plans might he have for me?" "Is it enough to live for myself?" Why or why not?

5. Bob Buford has said, "You can keep the box empty for only so long. If you do not choose the one thing that belongs in the box, life's inertia will choose it for you." What does he mean by this statement? How does it impact your halftime choices?

HALFTIME CLIP

Your "one thing" is the most essential part of you, your transcendent dimension. It is discovering what's true about yourself, rather than overlaying someone else's truth on you or injecting someone else's goals onto your personality. **—BOB BUFORD**

HALFTIME DRILL

What's in My Box?

Some of us, like Karol Emmerich, seem almost instinctively to know what belongs box. For others of us, it is a challenge to discover the one thing that belongs in the box. If you find yourself struggling to identify what belongs in your box, spend some time answering the following questions when this session is over. Be as specific as you can. You might know more about what's important to you than you realize!

What makes me tick?	
What is my passion, the spark that needs only a little breeze to ignite into a raging fire?	
What do I enjoy so much that I'd do it without pay?	
Which thing(s) outside my box have screamed for my attention?	
Where am I in my life now?	
Where do I want to be? What do I want to be doing in ten years? In twenty years?	
What gives me a deep sense of satisfaction and purpose?	
What do I feel I am missing in my life?	

Which God-given gifts have I perfected through the years?	
Which God-given gifts have I been unable to use much— or at all?	
What is difficult about choosing what's in my box—and living that way?	
Which regrets or mistakes may be holding me back from discovering what's in my box?	
What cause much bigger than my own personal concerns is worth living or dying for?	
What's in my box now? Do I want that to remain there?	
In what way(s) does my view of God influence what's in my box right now?	

Pause for Personal Reflection

Now it's time to pause to consider what might be in our respective boxes and to think about what God might be trying to say to each of us.

If someone asked me to reveal the one thing that motivates me, what would I say?

If my family members and/or friends were asked what motivates me, what would they say? How would their answers differ from mine?

How important a role do my core values and beliefs play in my daily decisions? (Be honest!)

How much time am I willing to devote to answering the question, "What's in my box?"

HALFTIME CLIP

No amount of activity will ever satisfy the longing to find the one thing that is uniquely yours—the thing that, once found, will enable you to make a difference.

—BOB BUFORD

SMALL GROUP EXPLORATION

Trusting God and His Leading

Bob Buford believes it's vital for people making the journey from success to significance to address the deeper spiritual issues. As we approach or find ourselves in halftime, we must carefully consider the role we will allow God to play in our lives. Will we trust him enough, for example, to ask him to guide us toward our calling and rejoice in the opportunity to pursue a significant second half?

Look up the following verses and discuss their implications for you as you move through the halftime process.

1. Psalm 46:1–3; Isaiah 40:28–31; 58:11

2. Psalm 29:11; Isaiah 26:3; Philippians 4:6–7

3. Proverbs 3:5–6; James 1:5–6

4. Lamentations 3:25; Matthew 7:7–11; James 5:16b–18; 1 John 5:14–15

5. Psalm 36:5; 1 Corinthians 1:9; Hebrews 10:23

6. Psalm 130:3–4; Colossians 2:13–15; 1 John 1:9

HALFTIME CLIP

Remember, you can have only one thing in the box. Regardless of your position in life, once you have identified what's in your box, you will be able to see the cluster of activities—surrounded by quiet times for spiritual disciplines, reading, and reflecting—that put into play your one thing and keep you growing.

—BOB BUFORD

Pause for Personal Reflection

Now it's time to pause to consider what role we will allow God to play as we go through halftime.

People in the video segment mentioned the importance of God in their lives. Am I actively seeking his calling for my life, or am I pursuing other things? As I evaluate what's in my box, where does God fit in?

What does my life look like from God's perspective? If God audibly spoke to me about my mission in life, what do I think he would say?

How is my view of God influencing my response to halftime?

Do I believe what the Bible says about God enough to risk discovering what he has for me during the second half of my life? Why or why not?

HALFTIME DRILL

In Which Spiritual-Belief Category Do You Fit?

As you seek to identify what belongs in your box and to explore the role your spiritual beliefs will play during your second half, it will be helpful to examine your level of spiritual belief and commitment and consider how it influences your halftime experience.

Which Spiritual-Belief Category Am I In?	How Is It Influencing My Goal to Discover What's in My Box?
Noncommitted. I believe in God, but seldom talk about it and rarely attend church. I am unfamiliar with the Bible.	
Creedal believer. I made a public acknowledgment of belief at one time and consider myself to be aligned with a religious movement or denomination. I attend church infrequently, usually on holidays.	
Active believer. I attend church regularly. I volunteer. I know quite a bit of religious teaching and have some biblical knowledge, but I am uncomfortable articulating my spiritual beliefs. I practice my religion within the church walls.	
Committed believer. I would describe my spiritual beliefs in terms of a personal relationship with God through Jesus Christ. I have a deeply spiritual life, regularly praying and reading the Bible. I'm comfortable talking about personal beliefs and helping other people learn more about their faith. I lead a life of service. I am active in church but don't equate church activities with a personal relationship with God.	

HALFTIME CLIP

Don't let the fact that you have to work for a living limit the grace God has in store for you during your second half. Don't allow the second half of your life to be characterized by decline, boredom, and increasing ineffectiveness for the kingdom. Listen carefully to that gentle whisper and then do some honest soul-searching. What's in your box? Is it money? Career? Family? Freedom?   **—BOB BUFORD**

GROUP DISCUSSION

Bob Buford writes, "The first half of life has to do with getting and gaining, learning and earning.... The second half is more risky because it has to do with living beyond the immediate. It is about releasing the seed of creativity and energy that has been implanted within us, watering and cultivating it so that we may be abundantly fruitful. It involves investing our gifts in service to others—and receiving the personal joy that comes as a result of that spending."

Deciding to put only one thing in the box is risky. Let's talk about some of those risks.

1. What are the risks of "releasing the seed of creativity and energy" that has been implanted within each of us? What might the benefits be?

2. Why do you think so much within our culture encourages us to use what we have been given—abilities, talents, financial means—to promote our own accomplishments and purposes rather than to serve other people?

3. What is the difference between being driven to achieve and being called purposefully toward one's destiny?

4. Do you agree or disagree with the statement, "The forces of evil would like nothing more than to prevent talented, productive people committed to God from becoming their truest selves in service to their Creator"? Why or why not?

ACTION POINTS

What will you commit to do as a result of what you have discovered during this session?

1. Each of us needs to identify and choose the one thing around which everything else in our life will flow. This mainspring is the source of our values and gives purpose to our lives. It is the overarching vision that shapes us and guides the investment of our talents, time, and treasure. Too often, people don't discover what's in the box and try to fill that void with pursuits that offer only temporary relief. That's why it is so important to clear a little space in our lives and discover the one thing that is most important to us.

    Take time now to think about what's in your box. Is it fame? Money? God? Family? Career?

    Perhaps you cannot yet write the one or two words that summarize what's in your box. If you are undecided, at least write down what you consider your options to be.

2. It's impossible to journey from success to significance without addressing deeper spiritual issues. As we approach or find ourselves in halftime, we must carefully consider the role we will allow God to play in our lives. Our view of God and our response to him color our view of the possibilities ahead of us and the level of our personal involvement. Thus it is important to establish a solid foundation of beliefs from which our attitudes, values, and actions will flow. That foundation begins with a personal relationship with God through Jesus Christ.

Set aside some quiet time to consider the following questions:

1. **In what way(s) am I satisfied and dissatisfied with my spiritual beliefs?**

2. **To what extent do my spiritual beliefs determine what I do and how I think? To what extent do they provide a solid foundation on which I can build a significant second half?**

3. For what do I need to trust God as I make a commitment to place my one thing in the box?

HALFTIME CLIP

I have hesitated, at times, to tell my story. I have been so uniquely blessed that I don't want anyone to conclude that only rich guys can have a better second half. Please remember that my second half is going well not because I have money but because I swallowed hard and put one thing in the box. It was not easy for me to do, nor will it be easy for you, either. But that is what has made the difference.

—BOB BUFORD

HALFTIME DRILL

What God Views as Significant

People try to find significance in various ways. We need only to look around us—and in our own lives—to see the consequences of those pursuits. Let's take a look at what God views as significant.

Look up the following verses and write out what they reveal about God's perspective on what's important.

Scripture	What God Views as Significant
Matthew 25:31–40; James 1:27	
Isaiah 57:15; Micah 6:8; Matthew 18:1–4; 23:12	
Leviticus 20:26; Psalm 97:10; Romans 13:12–14; 2 Timothy 2:19, 22	
Mark 12:28–31	
2 Timothy 4:7–8; Hebrews 11:6	
Matthew 5:38–47; Luke 6:32–35; Hebrews 13:16	
Psalm 11:7; 33:5; Jeremiah 9:24	

4

Game Plan for Significance

It is not enough to **feel** *like doing something significant. The newly discovered resolve that comes when you place just one thing in the box will fade if you do not apply it to a related goal.*

Bob Buford

QUESTIONS TO THINK ABOUT

1. What excites you most about the opportunities you are considering as a result of the halftime process?

2. What aspects of the halftime process seem a little intimidating or difficult at this point?

3. What do you want to do with the one thing you put into your box? What do you see as the next step to take?

HALFTIME CLIP

Most first-halfers become victims of centrifugal force. Around the perimeter of their lives are vital points that demand attention. ... They begin with every intention of tending to each, but in order to do that, they have to shift into a higher gear. Before long, they are spinning rapidly around the perimeter, the resulting force driving them farther and farther from the center, the core of who they are. **—BOB BUFORD**

VIDEO NOTES

Clare and Sue DeGraaf's wake-up call

A change of heart

Making a difference

Living life with no regrets

VIDEO HIGHLIGHTS

1. What role did Clare's view of God play in his journey from success to significance?

2. Once Clare got a taste of what it meant to allow God to guide his life, how did he respond? How might what happened to him relate to you?

3. Bob Buford knows about the risks of wrestling with the possibilities for significance. He observes, "In tossing aside the security blanket that keeps you safe and warm, you may have to set aside some familiar markers and reference points. You may feel, at least at first, that you're losing control of your life. To which I say, 'Good for you!'" What do you think he meant by this comment?

4. Clare views the activities of his second half as having eternal significance. What things do you view as having eternal significance?

HALFTIME CLIP

There will always be reasons to stay where you are. It is faith that calls you to move on. **—BOB BUFORD**

HALFTIME PERSPECTIVE

It's Time to Chart a New Course

- It may come on slowly—or almost demand to be addressed.
- It's about "a time to search and a time to give up" (Ecclesiastes 3:6).
- It's a time to search for new horizons and take on new challenges.
- It's a time to give up regrets.
- It's a time to start living by your own epitaph, perhaps daring to believe that what you ultimately leave behind will be more important than anything you could have possessed during your lifetime.
- It's a time to take risks because that's where the game is won or lost.
- It's about releasing the seeds of creativity and energy that have been implanted within you.
- It's about identifying yourself by internal standards—your character, your values, your beliefs, your contributions, your mission—rather than by your work, your possessions, your busyness, your children.
- It's about investing yourself in service to other people—and receiving the personal joy that comes as a result of that investment.
- It's about developing a mind-set, an inner compass, that is fixed on the things that define your true self as God has created you.

LARGE GROUP EXPLORATION

Developing a Personal Mission Statement

Perhaps you have already discovered what's in your box and feel enthusiastic about the opportunities for significance that you never dreamed existed. But it is not enough to feel like doing something significant. The newly discovered resolve that comes when you place just one thing into the box will fade if you don't apply it to a related goal. The time for good intentions is passed. It's time for each of us to develop a personal mission statement.

A personal mission statement defines what is most important to us and how we will arrange our priorities. It will help each of us define how we want our lives to count—what we will do and how we will go about doing it. It will release us to be ourselves and effectively use the gifts and talents we already possess.

1. What did you think or feel when you read or heard the words *personal mission statement?* Why?

2. What has been your previous experience with mission statements? Have you ever had a personal mission statement? If so, what did it accomplish for you? What do you see as the limitations or drawbacks of a mission statement?

3. Stephen Covey, author of *The Seven Habits of Highly Effective People*, suggests that when we develop a personal mission statement, we should focus on what we wish to be and do, based on the values and principles that undergird our beliefs and actions. What might some of the benefits be of approaching a mission statement this way as opposed to using other criteria?

4. Read the parable of the talents in Matthew 25:14–30. Bob Buford says, "The wonderful message from this story is that you and I will be held accountable only for what we were given, not for what others might have or expect from us. The guy who was given only two talents and doubled them was esteemed as highly as the guy who started out with five. We are not all given the same equipment, but we are expected to know what we were given and find ways to invest ourselves wisely."

    In what ways do you think developing a personal mission statement guides us in being better stewards of the talents God has given us?

Pause for Personal Reflection

What we've covered during the previous sessions has prepared us for taking action—for developing a personal mission statement. Now it's time to pause to reflect on what needs to go into that statement.

HALFTIME TIP

Peter Drucker suggests two important questions to help you discover the unique role God has prepared you to play:

1. What have you achieved? (This has to do with your competence.)
2. What do you care deeply about? (This has to do with your passion.)

If you look deeply enough inside yourself and are honest about combining your competence with your passion, you will find the mission that is best suited to you.

Write down several things I can do that are uniquely me, ambitious, and have a degree of risk.

In which would I like to make a real difference?

Which things have I done uncommonly well?

I probably have twenty-five or more productive years ahead of me. How do I want to spend them?

If I could accomplish nothing else, what are the top five things of significance I want to do before I die?

HALFTIME PERSPECTIVE

Tips for Choosing Your Life Mission

In addition to writing a personal mission statement, the halftime process involves choosing a life mission—usually selecting a specific task, cause, or organization—on which you will focus much of your time, talents, and resources during your second half. The following tips will help you begin pinpointing what your life mission will be.

1. Recognize how far you've already come in your journey toward significance. A key part of identifying your life mission is knowing who you are—your strengths, weaknesses,

aspirations, regrets, hopes, gifts. You already know what you have been given. Now it's time to find ways to invest yourself wisely.

2. Be patient with yourself. It will take time to work through your issues and plans. Don't jump into your life mission too fast. At the same time, don't be too patient to take the plunge.

3. Don't waste time and energy fantasizing about things that will never happen. Instead, face the tough questions so you can discover the real you.

4. Make lists of things you want to do—things to which you are committed, slogans and creeds that reflect the true you, statements that combine what you believe with what you want to do.

5. Seek out reliable counsel—trustworthy people with whom you can dialogue about your ideas. Ask them how they see you. Listen carefully to what they say and resist the temptation to be defensive. They can provide a fresh perspective on who you are and how God might use you during your second half.

6. Keep a journal as you seek your second-half mission. It will help you remember where you've been and clarify where you are headed. Writing out your thoughts also gives you the opportunity to see them on paper, where you can more easily review and evaluate them.

7. Prayer is a significant part of the halftime process. Psalm 139:23–24 reads, "Search me, O God, and know my heart; test me and know my anxious thoughts. See if there is any offensive way in me, and lead me in the way everlasting." God wants to help each of us examine our path and guide us toward our calling. He does not waste what he has built.

Continued on next page…

He didn't create you with specialized abilities and your unique temperament for no reason. God desires for you to serve him just by being who you are.

8. Before drilling for oil, an investor does seismic testing to see what an area may produce. Likewise, do your own seismic testing to get a little hands-on experience in something you may want to pursue. For example, assist someone in doing what you might like to do during your second half. Or take a short-term assignment. Or organize a focus group of people who are involved in your field of interest and ask them questions. If the exploratory results are negative, keep evaluating. You're saving yourself lots of trouble, expense, and time.

9. Consider doing what you currently do differently. Could you work fewer hours and invest yourself in a life mission that matters? Do you need to begin moving in a completely new direction? Are you ready to begin a parallel career?

10. Relax. Remember, what you do best for God will rise out of your core being—what God has created within you.

HALFTIME CLIP

I couldn't figure out why God would equip me as an entrepreneur, conceiver, starter, team builder, manager, and leader and then put me someplace where those things are worthless. I was relieved to discover that God does not waste what he has built. I am the same me I was in the first half, only applied to a different venue.　**—BOB BUFORD**

SMALL GROUP EXPLORATION

Clearing the Plate

Each of us has been taking steps that will lead toward significance. We have thought about many aspects of our lives and had to wrestle with challenging topics. Yet another part of the halftime process involves weeding out time- and energy-consuming activities that seem to control us but are not taking us where we want (and need) to go.

Unfortunately, many things—even good things—conspire to keep us where we've been and hinder our halftime journey. Thus it is important for us to recapture the majority of our time so we can use a portion of our time, talent, and treasure in discovering and pursuing our second-half mission.

1. In his parable about the farmer sowing seeds, Jesus shared truths that we can apply to halftime. Let's read Matthew 13:3–9 and think of ourselves—our lives, our dreams, our goals—as seeds that have the opportunity to grow and be fruitful.

   a. What kind of crop resulted from the seeds that fell onto good soil? What parallels might there be to our lives, to the impact each of us can have if we nurture what God has given us—our talents, resources, abilities?

   b. What things in life can scatter our potential in rocky places where there is little nourishment or choke out our innermost dreams and desires?

2. As a result of his spiritual commitment, Clare DeGraaf began learning about the Christian faith. He tested the waters of his future mission by sharing what he had learned with others. What big distraction did he need to clear out of his life in order to progress toward significance? What is involved in making that kind of commitment?

3. Bob Buford believes that each of us has social capital—time, money, and knowledge—that is available to reinvest or spend in the community that nurtures us. In what ways do you think our busy lives crowd out opportunities to share what God has given us?

4. A key element of the second half involves regaining control of our lives—calling our own shots. What are some reasons why it's important for each of us to slow down, return to the core of who we are, and recapture the majority of our time and other resources?

HALFTIME CLIP

Desire alone will not allow you to do something new in your second half; you must create the capacity to do it. If you are being controlled by too many time- and energy-consuming activities, you will continue to be frustrated by unfulfilled dreams and desires.

—BOB BUFORD

Pause for Personal Reflection

Now it's time to pause to consider how we will spend our time and resources in light of who we are, what's in our respective boxes, and our personal mission statements.

How willing am I:

- to consider how I spend my time?
- to determine which things need to have a higher priority and which things I can do less often or perhaps not at all?
- to make the necessary changes?

What are the relationships and activities in my life that demand my attention and compete for priority? Which of these may be keeping me from wrestling with who I am, what I profess to believe about my life, and what I can do to bring meaning and significance to my life?

If I were to reorder my time and priorities, rethink my vision of what life could be, look leisurely into the holiest chamber of my heart, and respond to my soul's deepest longings, what would my life be like? Where would I spend my time? What would I have to clear out of my life?

HALFTIME CLIP

Once we return to the core—once we know who we are and what's in the box—we can accept the fact that some of the things on the perimeter of our lives will not receive as much attention as they once did. Some things will be more important than others; some may need to be ignored altogether. But regardless of what stays and what gets tossed aside, the point is that we no longer let someone else decide that for us. We create the capacity for the things that matter.

—BOB BUFORD

HALFTIME DRILL

Time Priority Checklist

Once we identify the mainspring of our attitudes, beliefs, and actions and determine what should be in our personal mission statement, our best intentions to live a significant life may become buried beneath too many time- and energy-consuming activities.

Read the following checklist and start reassessing each priority in light of your halftime decisions and commitments. Write out the specific aspects of any priorities that you need to prune or to which you need to devote more time and energy.

Note: Pruning some priorities and nurturing others is a dynamic process. You may want to go through this checklist several times as you go through the halftime process. Your assessment is likely to be different every time.

Priority	Prune	Develop
Knowing God through a personal relationship with Jesus Christ		
Spending time with family members		
Developing friendships		
Hours I spend at or thinking about work		
Things on which I focus my mind		
Recreational activities		

Continued on next page...

Reading		
Praying		
Exercising		
Thinking about my life-related possibilities		
Forgiving myself and asking for God's forgiveness		
Assessing my strengths and weaknesses		
Taking time to dream about what could be		
Asking God for wisdom and strength		
Applying God's promises to my life		
Assessing my talents and treasures		
Thinking about my uniqueness		
Thinking about ways in which I could make an eternal difference		

GROUP DISCUSSION

1. Clare mentioned how God had changed the desires of his heart from loving business to loving ministry. In what ways has God been changing your heart since we started this series?

2. Learning new things is essential as we seek to take control of our lives in light of God's calling for us.

   a. What are some of the benefits of continuing to learn and acting on what we learn during the second half of our lives?

   b. Describe some ways in which we can keep on learning during the second half of our lives.

3. As it turned out, Clare's expertise in business prepared him to do exactly what God wanted him to do. In what ways is this an encouragement to you as you face the future?

HALFTIME CLIP

> *The feeling of being hurried is not usually the result of living a full life and having no time. It is, on the contrary, born of a vague fear that we are wasting our life. When we do not do the one thing we ought to do, we have no time for anything else—we are the busiest people in the world.*
>
> **—ERIC HOFFER**

ACTION POINTS

What will you commit to do as a result of what you have discovered during this session?

1. Defining what's in our box is an important step in the journey from success to significance. But unless our mission matches our intention, we will experience a dissonance that ultimately will be destructive. So it is essential that we each choose a mission and formulate a personal mission statement that matches whatever we put into our box. Once we have formulated our mission statement, we can begin to establish a game plan that will lead us in the direction we want to go.

   If you are ready to do so, write out your mission statement. Even if you are unsure of what it should be, at least write a proposed mission statement. Then set it aside for at least a week and follow the steps in the Halftime Drill below.

HALFTIME DRILL

Writing Your Mission Statement
Make lists of things to do during your second half, things you are committed to, slogans and creeds that reflect the true you, statements that combine what you believe with what you want to do with the rest of your life. After you have made your lists, pray. Read what you have written. Reflect. Listen. Share what you have written with your spouse and a small group of friends. Then put the paper away in a drawer. Pray some more. Listen a lot. Think about what you love to do the most, and let these thoughts roll gently through your soul like lazy waves on the ocean. After a week (or longer), write your mission statement.

2. We don't have to live life with regrets. Instead of just staying where we are and being afraid of change, each of us—no matter what our background may be—can take risks and step toward significance. We can clear our plate of distractions and unnecessary demands and start living out our personal life missions. We can embark on the journey of doing the good works God has ordained for us to do.

Now that you've written your proposed personal mission statement, how would you define your life mission?

Note: It should fit within your mission statement, and Bob Buford recommends that it be something ambitious that also has a degree of risk to it. When the odds are big and the task is demanding, you'll be drawn to contribute your best and release energies you didn't know you had.

Set aside several hours this week to think about:
- **The risks you may need to take.**
- **The changes you need to make to clear your plate of distractions.**
- **What you need to learn in order to keep moving toward significance.**

So you can begin living out your life mission.

HALFTIME PERSPECTIVE

Mission Statements

Many businesses and other organizations have developed mission statements, vision statements, or credos that attempt to explain why the company or organization exists and what it hopes to accomplish. When such declarations are well stated, they are usually easily understood and very simple. A mission statement becomes, as a team of consultants once noted in the *Harvard Business Review,* "the magnetic North Pole, the focal point" for that business. Everything the company or organization does points in that direction.

Developing a personal mission statement makes a lot of sense. In fact, you will not get very far in your second half without knowing your life mission. Can your mission be stated in a sentence or two?

A good way to begin formulating a mission statement is with some questions (and honest answers).

- What is your passion?
- What have you achieved?
- What have you done uncommonly well?
- How are you wired?
- Where do you belong?
- What are the "shoulds" that have trailed you during the first half?

These and other questions like them will direct you toward the self your heart longs for; they will help you discover the task for which you were especially made.

HALFTIME CLIP

My life mission is: To transform the latent energy in American Christianity into active energy.

This is what I do; it is how I want my life to count. It releases me to be myself—to use gifts that are already there. I do not have to become something that feels uncomfortable or strange. If your own mission statement fits you as well, it will be the right one for you. If it forces you into something that does not fit, it will be someone else's mission.

—BOB BUFORD

The Best of Your Years

To wake up every morning and feel as though you're where God wants you to be that day is as much peace as you're going to find this side of eternity.

Doug Mazza

QUESTIONS TO THINK ABOUT

1. During the first four sessions, we considered many aspects of halftime and wrestled with various challenges and issues. How has your view of the second half of life changed as a result? Must the second half be a period of decline and decay? Why or why not?

2. What happens to a person when he or she is able to make a significant difference in someone's life?

3. What impact would you like to make during your second half? Why do you think you can or cannot make such an impact?

4. In what ways do you think God can use what has happened during the first half of our lives to prepare us for the second?

VIDEO NOTES

The pursuit of blessedness

Relinquishing control

Discovering our passion—and going for it!

Making a significant difference

VIDEO HIGHLIGHTS

1. Bob Buford says, "The only way one can get to blessedness, I'm thoroughly persuaded, is to serve one another with the gifts that God has given us to work with." Do you agree or disagree? Why?

2. As the chief operating officer of Hyundai, Doug thought he had it made until his third son, Ryan, was born with severe deformities. Through his suffering, Doug reached the point where he prayed, "Lord, what is it that you would have me do next? I know you have prepared me for something more." What stood out to you as Doug shared his spiritual journey?

3. Why is it important for each of us, like Doug, to step out in faith to find the calling God has for us?

4. What attitudes do you see demonstrated in the people interviewed for this video? How successful have they been in
   encouraging you to find out what you're passionate about and
   to go for it?

LARGE GROUP EXPLORATION

Investing in People

God has given each of us some time, talent, and treasure to invest in fulfilling his two great commandments: "Love the Lord your God with all your heart and with all your soul and with all your mind.... Love your neighbor as yourself" (Matthew 22:37, 39). So as we each begin to chart a new course in life, we may want to think about partnering with God and investing our gifts in service to other people. There is nothing more rewarding than dedicating what we like to do and are good at doing in service to God and people.

1. More than two thousand years ago, Jesus demonstrated what it means to love people. He taught and ministered to crowds of people under the hot sun and experienced hunger and thirst. He lived in their world and walked their narrow streets. He gave himself—his time, resources, wisdom, knowledge, power, and ultimately his life—for the benefit of other people, even those who hated him. And no one in the history of the world has done anything as significant as he did (and is still doing!).

   Let's look up the following verses and see what they reveal about Jesus' love for people and what it means for us to love the people around us—at home, at work, in our communities.

Scripture	How Jesus Loved People in His World	How We Might Love People in Our World
Matthew 8:1–3		
Matthew 20:29–34		
Luke 5:27–32		
John 8:1–11		
John 11:1–6, 17, 32–44		

2. Let's list some practical ways in which we can use who we are and our resources to demonstrate God's love to other people.

HALFTIME PERSPECTIVE

Altruistic Egoism

In *Halftime*, Bob Buford mentioned that Hans Selye coined a phrase that sounds contradictory: *altruistic egoism.* It means that helping other people helps you. This truth is nothing new. Long ago, Jesus taught that giving of one's self to other people is actually a form of receiving (Acts 20:35).

Selye noted that people who earn their neighbors' goodwill are dramatically better off psychologically and physically than those who are looked upon as selfish and greedy. He also wrote that the best way to earn the goodwill of your neighbor is to ask either explicitly or implicitly, "What can I do to be useful to you?" And then, if possible, do it.

Pause for Personal Reflection

Now it's time to pause to consider how God may want us to use our gifts and what we are passionate about in loving service to other people.

If God audibly spoke to me about my mission in life related to people, what would he say? Why?

Jesus spent the last three years of his life in public ministry, reaching out to people with God's love. In what ways has the first half of my life prepared me, given my options and uniqueness, knowledge and experience, to reach out to other people?

In what ways might I be able to use what I've been given to serve other people?

I typically respond to needy, hurting people by _____

_____

_____.

What does this tell me about my role in serving other people?

To which people, or group of people, may God be calling me to love and serve in a special way?

HALFTIME CLIP

This is the true joy in life—the being used for a purpose recognized by yourself as a mighty one, the being a force of nature instead of a feverish, selfish little clod of ailments and grievances, complaining that the world will not devote itself to making you happy. I am of the opinion that my life belongs to the whole community and as long as I live, it is my privilege to do for it whatever I can. I want to be thoroughly used up when I die, for the harder I work, the more I live.

—GEORGE BERNARD SHAW

SMALL GROUP EXPLORATION

Living by Our Inner Compass

Bob Buford has observed that "the halftime process of reevaluation is about identifying yourselves by internal standards—your
character, your values, your beliefs, your contributions, your mission—rather than by your work, your possessions, your busyness, your children." An internal approach is purpose driven, not
driven by external circumstances. This observation echoes the
words of Moses in Deuteronomy 30:20. He implored the Israelites
to identify themselves by an internal standard, to "love the LORD
your God, listen to his voice, and hold fast to him. For the LORD
is your life."

A similar sentiment was expressed by Mihaly Csikszentmiha-
lyi, a psychologist who spent twenty-five years trying to figure out
what makes people happy. He discovered that happiness doesn't
just happen, nor does it have much to do with power, money, or
material possessions. "People who control inner experience," he
observed, "will be able to determine the quality of their lives,
which is as close as any of us can come to being happy."

Since significance and quality of life are such important ingredients in making our second-half years the best of our years, let's
consider some biblical passages that call us to exercise discipline
over our inner selves and live according to internal standards.

1. What do the following verses reveal about how we each set
    our inner compass, how we determine the inner standards
    that, with God's help, will lead toward a more fulfilled, signif-
    icant life?

    a. Matthew 6:24–25, 31–34

b. Romans 8:5–8

2. It takes discipline to exercise control and live according to our inner compass. Read the instructions given in the following Scripture passages. Note what is said regarding our ability to exercise control over our lives.

a. 1 Timothy 6:12; 2 Timothy 2:1, 3–5

b. 1 Corinthians 9:24–27

c. Hebrews 12:1

d. 1 Peter 1:13–15

3. In light of the passages we've read above, let's talk for a
    minute about the importance of living by our inner compass
    and how we go about controlling our inner experiences. What
    impact do you think living this way will have on our second
    half? On living a significant life?

Pause for Personal Reflection

Now it's time to pause to think quietly about our lives and consider how we each set our inner compass.

Lloyd Reeb said, "My real significance at the end of the day is
not so much about my effectiveness as it is about my willingness
to follow and partner with God where he has called me."

Is this statement motivated by internal or external standards?

How would I describe the source of my significance? Is my
significance internally or externally motivated?

On a scale of one to ten, how would I rate my control of my inner experience? What changes do I need to make to better focus my inner compass on things that reflect my true self, the self God created me to be?

As I look at my daily schedule, is there room in my life for anything else? If not, what do I need to eliminate so that I can carve out more time for things that better represent my core being?

HALFTIME CLIP

Having a fruitful second half is more than just slowing down or being able to control your date book. It has to do with a mind-set, an inner compass, that is fixed on those things that define the true self.

—BOB BUFORD

HALFTIME TIP

Ten Principles for Regaining Control of Your Life

As Bob Buford pointed out in his book *Halftime*, it's one thing to talk about regaining personal control, yet quite another to really do it. Old habits, even tempered with a brand-new outlook on life, die hard. The following list summarizes how Buford regained control over his destiny. Perhaps some of these principles will apply to you.

1. *Delegate—at work, play, and home.* You cannot do everything and shouldn't try. This is especially important if you keep your present job but do it at half speed so you can express yourself in other ways. Work smarter, not harder.

2. *Do what you do best; drop the rest.* Go with your strengths.

3. *Know when to say no.* The more successful you are, the more you'll be asked to help other people. Don't get talked into doing something you don't want to do or don't have time to do. Pursue your mission, not someone else's.

4. *Set limits.* Cut back on your appointments, your work time, your business trips. Reallocate time to your life mission.

5. *Protect your personal time by putting it on your calendar.* Start your day slowly. It's much easier to maintain control over your life if you have a regular quiet time. A quiet time is more than Bible reading and prayer. Allow time for absolute silence, for deliberately looking at your life to see if it's in balance.

6. *Work with people you like.* As much as possible, work with people who add energy to life, not those who take energy away.

7. *Set timetables.* Your life mission is important, deserving of your attention and care. Second-half dreams that are not put on a timetable quickly become unfulfilled wishes.

Continued on next page...

8. *Downsize.* To what extent are your time and energy being drained by owning a boat, a cottage, a third car, or a country club membership? None of these things are bad in and of themselves, but if these things stand between you and regaining control of your life, get rid of them.

9. *Play more often.* Play ought to be a big second-half activity, not so much in terms of time spent, but in importance. Play will remind you who's in charge.

10. *Take the phone off the hook.* Learn how to hide gracefully. Unless you're a brain surgeon on twenty-four-hour call, it's not necessary to let people know where you are all the time. Answering machines and voice mail allow us to control who we talk with—and when.

HALFTIME PERSPECTIVE

Three Truths to Remember

1. *What we become during the second half has already been invested during the first half.* We don't have to worry about trying to recreate ourselves. We can examine where we've been and would like to go, and build on our experiences, talents, and knowledge in pursuing our God-given calling.

2. *We don't need to chase things outside of ourselves for fulfillment.* Many people have pursued power, money, possessions, status, and the like, believing that these things would lead to significance. But what's really important is knowing God through a personal relationship with Jesus Christ, discovering the calling God has for each of us, and receiving the blessedness that comes from serving other people.

3. *God doesn't waste what he has created.* God created each of us just the way we are! He desires that we serve him by being who we are and using what he has given us to work with. Not only that, he offers us his love, wisdom, guidance, and strength—all the ingredients we need for a significant second half.

GROUP DISCUSSION

1. In what ways has your view of yourself and your role in the second half of your life changed since we began this study?

HALFTIME CLIP

I like to think of halftime as an opportunity, sort of a renaissance. Listen, learn, and do it! The worst you could do is to have to try again.
—RENA PEDERSON

2. We've learned a lot about ourselves during our times together. Yet what we've learned is just the beginning. Continuing to learn and grow is a crucial part not only of our halftime experience but also of our second half. Learning and growing are key ingredients in making the rest of our years the best of our years.

    In what ways may we need to learn and grow during our second half? In what ways is the learning process different during our second half than it was during our first half? How do we go about learning during our second half?

3. Bob Buford used the Sigmoid Curve to illustrate a pattern of learning and growth that will sustain us through life. (See Halftime Perspective: Overlapping Curves of Growth on page 121.) Why is it so important for each of us to assess how we use our time and other resources and to start a new curve before the last one peters out?

HALFTIME CLIP

The mistake most people make when they move into the second half is to rely on good intentions. If, at some point, you become discouraged by lack of progress in your life mission, it is possible that you simply may not have gained the knowledge and information necessary to support your dream.... In many ways, everything that you do in the second half is a form of learning. That is because learning is really just adopting an attitude of discovery. Expect to learn from everything you approach and don't get too hung up on trying to formalize your study.

—BOB BUFORD

HALFTIME PERSPECTIVE

Overlapping Curves of Growth

Everything, according to Bob Buford, conspires to keep us where we are. That is why so many people remain stuck in the first half or, at best, flounder in a perpetual halftime. Life seems more comfortable in known, familiar territory, even when it bores us to tears and we are fairly certain something better awaits us out there.

How can we overcome this holding pattern? Charles Handy, in his book *The Age of Paradox,* offers a solution: to keep learning and growing into something new. He illustrates this growth pattern in what he has labeled the Sigmoid Curve (see diagram).

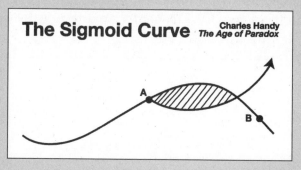

"The secret to constant growth," Handy says, "is to start a new Sigmoid Curve before the first one peters out. The right place to start that second curve is at Point A, where there is the time, as well as the resources and energy, to get the new curve through its initial explorations and flounderings before the first curve begins to dip downward."

The normal pattern for most people, according to Buford, is a single curve that rises as we approach middle age, then sharply drops off toward retirement. A much better approach to life is to have a series of overlapping curves, each one beginning before the previous curve is played out. Buford describes the overlapping curves of his life like this:

The First Curve	The Second Curve
school	apprentice work
apprentice work	doing work
doing work	leading work
leading work	doing ministry
doing ministry	leading ministry
leading ministry	portfolio of ministries

Where are you right now? Are you stuck in one place? Are you just doing time while your first curve drops off? Don't wait to be finished with what you are doing before you start the next curve. You'll always have reasons to stay put. It is faith that calls you to move on.

ACTION POINTS

What will you commit to do as a result of what you have discovered during this session?

1. Jesus said, "It is more blessed to give than to receive" (Acts 20:35). When we have a dynamic, personal relationship with God through Jesus Christ, we can use our God-given gifts to serve other people, and we'll receive blessedness in return. Nothing we can do is more exciting or significant than partnering with God in a spirit of trust and obedience and using the gifts he has given us to do what he has called us to do on behalf of other people.

    Carefully think through the people God has brought into your life with whom you have a special desire to share your talents, knowledge, wisdom, etc.

    What practical steps can you begin taking to explore your options for giving of yourself to other people?

2. Halftime is the time to begin living life out of our core being—out of our internal standards such as character, values, beliefs, and mission—rather than by our work, possessions, accomplishments, and children. We can apply proven principles and biblical truths in order to regain control of our lives and experience the significance that comes from living out God's calling.

    Spend some quiet time during the coming weeks drawing closer to God. Focus on knowing God, discovering who he made you to be, and seeking his will for your life through

Bible reading, prayer, and discussions with other Christians.

Begin writing out the decisions you can make, the steps of faith you can take that will help you take charge of your inner life.

If you have not accepted Jesus Christ as your Lord and Savior, talk with a Christian friend or local pastor to learn more about how you can have a personal relationship with God.

3. Learning and growing are not just key ingredients of the halftime process. They remain crucial parts of life during the second half. Learning and growing are part of what sustains us through life. As we challenge ourselves to keep pursuing what we are passionate about, tap into our gifts, and seek—with God's help—to discover his calling for each of us, the rest of our years will be the best of our years!

    Compare your life's curves to a Sigmoid Curve. Are you stuck in the first half? Are you on the verge of a downward slide? Are you on the upward slope of a new curve?

    Identify where you are on your present curve and consider when you need to begin the next curve. Describe what the focus of that learning and growth curve will be.

HALFTIME CLIP

Eventually your first half will end. The clock will run out. If it happens unexpectedly—if you do not take responsibility for going into half-time and ordering your life so that your second half is better than the first, you will join the ranks of those who are coasting their way to retirement.... But if you take responsibility for the way you play out the rest of the game, you will begin to experience the abundant life that our Lord intended for you.   **—BOB BUFORD**

HALFTIME TIP

Three Principles for Living Out the Best of Your Years

Peter Drucker, noted business writer and consultant, taught Bob Buford three cardinal principles that have helped him keep control over his life:

1. *Build on the islands of health and strength.* You'll build independence rather than dependence.

2. *Work only with those who are receptive to what you are trying to do.* Sure, situations arise in which you can't always do this. But remember, you have only a limited amount of time. Trying to convince people to do what they don't want to do uses four times the energy required to help someone conceive or implement their own ideas.

3. *Work only on things that will make a great deal of difference if you succeed.*

HALFTIME PERSPECTIVE

A Final Challenge

When I look across the Christian landscape in America, I see a powerful reservoir of energy just waiting to be unleashed. I see enough talent, creativity, compassion, money, and strength to transform our culture.... Yet the church will never have credibility in the community at large without *expressed* individual responsibility. People need to *see* our faith, not merely hear about it.

When our beliefs are personal and privatized, practiced only inside a building once a week, we Christians miss out on that glorious opportunity to be salt and light. Worse, I believe that when faith continues to be directed inward, we become one-dimensional, uninteresting, and wholly self-centered persons.

In the final analysis, you alone must choose how you want to live. You have the freedom to decide whether or not you want the rest of your years to be the *best* of your years. My prayer for you is that you will have the courage to live the dreams God has placed within you.

See you after the game.

—Bob Buford

Other Resources by Bob Buford

Halftime
Changing Your Game Plan from Success to Significance

"There are hundreds of books about how to make a living, but only a few about how to make a life. I wanted to write a book about how I shifted the primary loyalty in my life to Significance without abandoning the satisfactions of Success," says Bob Buford. In this popular book, he guides men through times of reflection and re-evaluation, to help them clarify values and establish goals that will help them lead a more significant life—a life where they become all God created them to be.

Hardcover
0-310-37540-1
Softcover
0-310-21532-3

n *Halftime,* Buford focuses on the important time of transition—the time when, s he says, a person moves beyond the first half of the game of life. It's halftime, a me of revitalization. A time for catching new vision for living the second, most rewarding half of life.

Game Plan
Winning Strategies for the Second Half of Your Life

ame *Plan* takes men, individually or in groups, through a ries of steps that help them evaluate where they are, determine where they are most suited to go, and develop a plan at will take them there. Personal inventories, activities,

Softcover
0-310-22908-1

d assignments help a man apply the Halftime principles directly to his unique rsonality and gifts. They help him develop a strategy that will work—one that ll help him make a lasting impact on the world by being exactly who God created him to be.

Game Plan, Buford gives you a practical way to move from success to significance—and create an individual strategy that can get you where you want to be e...ten...twenty...thirty...or more years from now.

Also look for...
Halftime/Game Plan Audio Pages
ISBN: 0-310-21583-8

Pick up your copies today at your local bookstore!

Please send your comments about this book to us
in care of the address below. Thank you.

ZondervanPublishingHouse
Grand Rapids, Michigan 49530
http://www.zondervan.com